Y0-EGE-997

This book is dedicated to the honor and glory of our Lord and Savior, Jesus Christ.

This book is a celebration of my precious adult children: Andrés, Selah & Nate, and Cloudi!

I love you with all my heart!

In Honor of Steven Hamilton, Bill & Mildred DeShazo, Sharon & Ladell Kirk, Vurl Emeory Bland III, and Ernie Hill.

In Loving Memory of Glenda Bland, Elaine Bland, Vurl Bland, Vurlenda Hill, and James & Betty Hamilton.

To find more sign language materials and or to find out how you can support our mission efforts contact Expressions of Emmanuel.
Website: www.expressionsofemmanuel.com
Facebook: Expressions of Emmanuel
YouTube: ExpressionsEmmanuel
Email: vondabland@msn.com.

Heart to Heart Publishing, Inc.

PO Box 50644
Bowling Green, KY 42102
(270) 526-5589
www.hearttoheartpublishinginc.com

Copyright© 2020
Publishing Rights: Heart to Heart Publishing, Inc.
Library of Congress Control No. 2020923746
ISBN 978-1-937008-02-4

Author: Vonda Bland Hamilton
Artist: Samantha Smith
Designer: April Yingling-Jernigan

Printed in USA

First Edition
Heart to Heart Publishing, Inc. books are available at a special discount for bulk
purchases in the US by corporations, institutions, and other organizations. For more
information, please contact Special Sales at 270-526-5589.

Scriptures were taken from the below sources
and may have been adapted for the target audience.
Quotations marked "NIV" reference:
HOLY BIBLE, NEW INTERNATIONAL VERSION® NIV®. Copyright© 1973, 1978,
1984 by International Bible Society. Used by permission of Zondervan.
All rights reserved.

Quotations marked "NCV" reference:
New Century Version. Copyright© 1987, 1988, 1991 by Thomas Nelson, Inc.
Used by permission. All rights reserved.

Quotations marked "NLT" reference:
Holy Bible, New Living Translation. Copyright© 1996, 2004, 2007, 2013, 2015 by
Tyndale House Foundation. Used by permission of Tyndale House Publishers, Inc.
All rights reserved.

Quotations marked "VOICE" reference:
The Voice™. Copyright© 2012 by Ecclesia Bible Society.
Used by permission. All rights reserved.

Quotations marked "WEV" reference:
THE JESUS BOOK – The Bible in Worldwide English – New Testament. Copyright©
1996 by SOON Education Publications. Used by permission.

Quotations marked "ERV" reference:
HOLY BIBLE: EASY-TO-READ VERSION. Copyright© 2001 by Bible League
International. Used by permission.

"Vonda Hamilton and Samantha Smith have created a beautifully
illustrated and biblically integrated way to learn the meaning
of idioms. English as a Second Language students, Deaf students,
and all children will enjoy the illustrations and the connection
to God's word. Teachers will be blessed with this book as a
classroom resource for teaching some of the strange
phrases we use in English. Vonda has been teaching and
ministering to the Deaf and to deaf children for many years and
makes the Word of God come alive in American Sign Language
and Samantha's illustrations delightfully entertain on each page."

- Jan Pride
Executive Director at Happy Hands Education Center
Tulsa, Oklahoma

Cloudi Bland, 2001-2002

Thanks be to my Lord and Savior, Jesus, for His love and for the creative ideas that He gives.

What a joy to write this book for kids and especially for Deaf kids!
I am so thankful my mother inspired me to write so many years ago! I know she and other family members are among
the great cloud of witnesses in heaven cheering me on!
Thanks to my precious husband who always supports me and believes in the creativity that God gives me.
I am thankful for my three children to whom I taught lots of idioms. As Deaf youth, Andrés and Cloudi showed me how important
and fun it is for Deaf children to learn idioms! Thank you! I am thankful for Selah and Nate as they reaffirmed God's calling for me to
write books.
Thanks to Selah for her creative thoughts and editing help.
I am so thankful for Sharon and Rick Reece, Jackina Stark, Kathy Christophel, and Sharon and Ladell Kirk for challenging me to write,
sharing ideas, and helping edit.
My brother, Emeory (Vurl), and his girlfriend, Ginny, were also a huge encouragement as they let me share the vision for the book.
They totally believed it would be a fun and helpful learning tool. I am also thankful for Jan Pride's friendship, her faith,
and her support for this project.
Thanks to LATM and many others for their support of this book. Thanks to Sam, Martha, Chan White, and family for their support of
this book. The Whites gave in memory of Bertis White, their beloved father and husband, a precious man of God.
A big back scratch to the dogs and cats of our family: Luna, Neo, River, Hazelnut, Miss Kitty, Black Belt, and Anne.
Finally, these concepts would not really make sense without a great artist. I'm so thankful for Samantha Smith and her faith, patience,
perseverance, sign language/language knowledge, Christlike attitude, and great artistic ability!
Thanks to all and glory to God!

Vonda

MISS KITTY

BLACK BELT   LUNA

NEO

ANNE

RIVER

HAZELNUT

The APPLE doesn't fall far from the tree.

Meaning: A child has a similar characteristic, talent, quality, or habit like one or both of their parents.

We need to be like God, our Father.

1 John 2:6 "Whoever says that he lives for God must live as Jesus lived." NCV

BIRDS of a feather flock together.

Meaning: People who enjoy the same things will meet together.

Bad friendship will cause troubles. Good friendship will bring peace.

1 Corinthians 15:33 "Do not be fooled: Bad friends will ruin good habits." NCV

CAT got your tongue?

Meaning: This question is asked when someone is exceptionally quiet and does not speak up.

We must speak/sign to help others.

Proverbs 31:8-9 "Speak up for those who cannot speak for themselves; defend the rights of all those who have nothing. Speak up and judge fairly and defend the rights of the poor and needy." NIV

Dd

Shake it off like water off a DUCK's back.

Meaning: People don't let mean words hurt them, but they just ignore the unkind words, continue to be kind, and refuse to become bitter.

When someone is mean to you or picks on you, try to live at peace with them. Don't try to get even with others, but let God take care of it.

Romans 12:17 "Do not repay anyone evil for evil. Be careful to do what is right in the eyes of everyone. Do not get even or be mean to get back to others, let God take care of people who are mean." NIV

Size comparison

Ee

Your EYES are bigger than your stomach.

Meaning: A person takes too much food, so much food that they cannot eat it.

We don't want to be selfish and make ourselves sick by eating too much food.

Proverbs 23:20b -21 "Don't eat too much food. Those who drink and eat too much become poor, they sleep too much and end up wearing rags." NCV

Cold FEET

Ff

Meaning: If someone has "cold feet" that means that they are too afraid to get started to do something. Having "cold feet" means to be fearful, lack courage and confidence. If a man or woman is afraid to go to their wedding to get married, then they have "cold feet".

God wants His children not to be afraid to work for God.

Isaiah 41:10 "So don't worry, because I am with you. Don't be afraid, because I am your God. I will make you strong and will help you; I will support you with my right hand that saves you." NCV

Gg

Go for the GOLD.

Meaning: This is when your goal is to do your very best.

We need to do our best in all we do to honor God.

Romans 12:11 "Do not be lazy but work hard, serving the Lord with all your heart." NCV

Hh   Hold your HORSES.

Meaning: Places are crowded or things are very full!

God will give abundant blessings to His children!

Deuteronomy 28:12a "The Lord will open the heavens to send rain on your land and to bless all the work of your hands." NIV

He's a real KNIGHT in shining armor.

Meaning: He is someone who is kind, brave, and helps you in hard times.

Helmet of Salvation

Breastplate of Righteousness

Shield of Faith

Belt of Truth

Gospel Shoes of Peace

Sword of the Spirit

Christians need to be kind and help others. Christians need the full armor of God to be strong and kind.

Ephesians 6: 10-11 (12-17) "Finally be strong in the Lord and in His great power. Put on the full armor of God so that you can fight against the devil's evil tricks."
"Belt of truth, breastplate of right living, the Good News shoes of peace,
shield of faith, the helmet of salvation, and the Sword of the Spirit which is the Word of God." NCV

He's really sawing LOGS!

MEANING: A person is sleeping very well and probably snoring.

When we trust in God, we can sleep well, because we know that God is taking care of us.

Proverbs 3:24 "When you lie down, you will not be afraid; when you lie down, your sleep will be sweet." NIV

He has a MILK TOAST personality.

MEANING: People with a milk toast personality are easily picked on, are not very sure of themselves, and normally don't do a good job. A milk toast personality is someone who is wishy washy or "riding the fence" about life and decisions.

We need to be brave, obey God, and live for Him. When we trust Jesus we don't need to be afraid. God will help us to be bold and strong like a lion.

Proverbs 28:1 "The wicked (bad people) run away when no one is chasing them, but the righteous (God's children) are bold and strong as a lion." VOICE

Nn

NIP it in the bud.

MEANING: "Nip it in the bud" means to quickly stop doing evil or bad.

God wants us to stop doing bad or evil and to do what is right.

1 Corinthians 15:34 "Wake up, do what is right, and stop sinning!" WEV

Oo

You're an ODD duck!

MEANING: You are an unusual person. You are different than other people.

God wants His children to obey, live right, and be different than people who just want to do wrong.

1 Peter 2:9-10 "You are a chosen people, a royal priesthood, a holy nation, God's special people, that you may tell the praises of Jesus who called you out of darkness into His wonderful light." NIV

You are two PEAS in a POD!

MEANING: It means that two people are a lot alike or they are very close.

God wants His children, members of His church, to be close and get along together in unity. We need to be close friends in God's family. We need to help and love each other.

Proverbs 18:24 "There are "friends" who destroy each other, but a real friend sticks closer than a brother." NLT

Mind your P's and Q's.

MEANING: Mind your P's and Q's means to be on your best behavior, to be careful about what you are doing, to use good language, and to use good manners.

If we love God, then we will obey, use good manners, and use good words. If we love God, then we will carefully remember God's Word, the Bible. We will want to obey the Bible.

John 14:23 Jesus said, "If people love Me, then they will obey My teaching." NCV

You're a RAY of sunshine!

MEANING: If you are called "a ray of sunshine" that means that you are a joyful happy person. When someone brings hope and joy to others, they are called a ray of sunshine.

God commands us to rejoice. God wants His children to be joyful. God's joy gives us strength and helps us bring hope to others.

Nehemiah 8:10 b "The joy of the Lord is your strength." NIV

You're SAILING right along.

MEANING: It means to continue traveling or moving steadily. When someone is working on a job and they continue getting more work done, little bit by little bit, step by step… then they are "SAILING right along."

When we trust and obey God, He will help us with our work. If we are steadily faithful in a little job, God will trust us to do bigger jobs. If we do not do a good job and do not tell the truth about little things, we will not do good work and be truthful about big jobs.

Luke 16:10 "Whoever can be trusted with a little can also be trusted with a lot, and whoever is dishonest with a little is dishonest with a lot." NCV

MEANING: "To Talk Turkey" means to talk straightforward, honestly, and openly about something.

God wants us to tell the truth. God does not want us to lie. God wants us to speak to others with love even when we talk about things that are hard to talk about. God smiles when we speak the truth in love.

Ephesians 4:15a "Speak the truth with love." NIV

UNDER the weather

MEANING: When someone feels a little sick or sad, then they are feeling "Under the Weather."

God's children can become sick and sad, but God wants to heal our bodies and our hearts.
We need to pray and ask God to heal us.

Jeremiah 17:14 "Heal me, Lord, and I will be healed; save me and I will be saved, for you are the one that I praise." NIV

MEANING: This is when someone is mean and selfish with a person who is having problems. Just like a vulture eats wounded and or dead animals, a person can be like a vulture when they are unkind to others.

God wants His children to treat other people with love and respect. God's children must be fair to others.

Proverbs 22:22 a & 23a "Do not abuse poor people because they are poor…. The Lord will defend them." NCV

Ww

You WAKE UP with the chickens!

MEANING: This is when a person wakes up really early in the morning at or before sunrise.

When we wake up in the morning, we need to pray to God. God will guide our day. It is best to ask God to help guide you early in the day.

Psalm 143:8 "Tell me in the morning about your love, because I trust You. Show me what I should do, because my prayers go up to you." NCV

X marks the spot.

Xx

MEANING: X marks the spot means that this is the exact location or the exact area where the thing that you are searching for can be found.

God wants our hearts. Every person has a heart that needs God. Just like a pirate uses a map to search for hidden treasure, God's children need to seek God's Word, the Bible, and trust in God! When we seek, find, and welcome God into our hearts, then our hearts will be full and that is exactly what we need!

Matthew 6:33 "But seek first and want most God's kingdom and what God wants. Then all the other things that you need will be given to you." NCV

YOU can catch more flies with honey, than with vinegar.

MEANING: You can get more help when you are kind and polite than when you are rude or mean.

God wants us to be kind. God's children can do so much more good work when we are kind to each other and work in unity.

Proverbs 16:24 "Kind words are like honey -- sweet to the soul and healthy for the body." NLT

A ZEBRA cannot change its stripes.